WOLVES

SIERRA CLUB
WILDLIFE
LIBRARY

WOLVES

by R. D. Lawrence

Sierra Club Books
San Francisco

Little, Brown and Company
Boston • Toronto • London

The Sierra Club, founded in 1892 by John Muir, has devoted itself to the study and protection of the earth's scenic and ecological resources—mountains, wetlands, woodlands, wild shores and rivers, deserts and plains. The publishing program of the Sierra Club offers books to the public as a nonprofit educational service in the hope that they may enlarge the public's understanding of the Club's basic concerns. The Sierra Club has some sixty chapters in the United States and in Canada. For information about how you may participate in its programs to preserve wilderness and the quality of life, please address inquiries to Sierra Club, 730 Polk Street, San Francisco, CA 94109.

First Edition

Photo credits:

© Bill Ivy, 9; © Jacana/The Image Bank, 62; © Edgar T. Jones, 8; © Scott Leslie/First Light, 46; © Peter McLeod/First Light, 5, 7, 12, 13, 25, 32, 35, 37, 41, 50-51; © L. David Mech, 26, 27, 28, 29, 30, 31, 34, 39, 45, 59; © Dennis W. Schmidt, 11, 20, 40; © Esther Schmidt, 3, 38, 42; © U.S. Fish and Wildlife Service, 19; © U.S. National Park Service, 23; © Terry Willis, 56, 60; © Art Wolfe, 1, 22, 49, 61; © Art Wolfe/Image Bank, 18

Library of Congress Cataloging-in-Publication Data

Lawrence, R. D., 1921–
    Wolves / by R.D. Lawrence — 1st ed.
       p.   cm. — (Sierra Club wildlife library)
    Summary: Follows the life cycle of wolves, from their birth, through their early months of growth and development, to their daily lives as adults.
    Includes index.
    ISBN 0-316-51676-7
    1. Wolves — Juvenile literature.   [1. Wolves.]   I. Title.
II. Series.
QL737.C22L36   1990
599.74'442—dc20   90-8730

Sierra Club Books/Little, Brown children's books are published by Little, Brown and Company (Inc.) in association with Sierra Club Books.

10 9 8 7 6 5 4 3 2 1

Published simultaneously in Canada by
Key Porter Books Limited

Printed in Singapore

Contents

A Ring of Wolves

Eight timber wolves surrounded me, howling eerily. I was convinced that they meant to kill and eat me. Fear made my mouth go dry.

I had been kneeling in the January snow preparing to cut down a spruce tree when I first heard crackling sounds, made—I thought—by a harmless animal traveling through the forest. Before I could even look up, two wolves began to howl. They were very near. Moments later, the other wolves in the pack raised their voices.

Suddenly, they became silent. I looked up then and saw one wolf, a large gray animal, come from between two trees and stare at me. Its yellow eyes looked right through me before it disappeared behind the trees. "Good, they're going away," I thought. Instead, they began to circle me again and once more sent up that fierce howling.

Putting down my saw and picking up my ax, I backed toward a pile of spruce logs that I had stacked the previous day, for I was cutting pulpwood for a paper mill. With my back against the pile, I prepared to defend myself. The wolves continued to run around me and kept on howling.

Then I saw three of them. They had stopped and were only about eight feet away. The big one I'd seen earlier, who I believed was one of the leaders of the pack, stared at me again, but now he wrinkled his lips and showed his huge yellow fangs. He then growled, a loud, ferocious sound that made the hairs on the back of my neck stand up.

I was sure I was going to be killed out there in the wilderness of northern Canada, far from any other human. And I imagined how my body would be torn apart and eaten, and how my gory bones

Wolf packs rarely attack humans. They usually try to avoid contact with people.

would be left scattered for the ravens and gray jays to pick at.

On the ground at my feet, I saw a piece of spruce about four feet long and two inches thick. I picked it up, thinking I could use it as a club. Then I climbed on top of the log pile, which was about six feet high. Now I had a better view. I could count the wolves, and I noticed that it was the really big one that always came closest to me.

The wolves continued to circle, howling as loud as ever, but now and then barking—sounds not quite the same as the barking of dogs. Soon now, I told myself, they will attack. But they didn't. One black wolf was, I thought, a female, perhaps the mate of the big gray leader.

A wolf's paw print is about the size of a man's hand.

Still they did not rush to attack. I couldn't stand the tension any longer. With the ax in one hand and the club in the other, I jumped off the log pile and, without bothering to put on my snowshoes, walked shakily to the entrance of my trail.

If I could get through the ring of wolves, I would go to find my neighbor, who was logging about a mile and a half away. Early that morning, before the sun had climbed over the trees, I had stopped to chat with him and noticed that he had brought along his rifle. Perhaps, if I reached him safely, I could borrow his gun and return to shoot my tormentors.

Like people, wolves have expressive faces.

I made myself walk through that ring of wolves. As I entered my trail, I saw three of them only about six feet from me. To my surprise, however, they still did not try to attack.

Once through the ring, I walked as fast as I could, but I wasn't able to resist looking back every now and then. When I had gone about two hundred yards, the wolves stopped howling. Now would they chase after me and kill me? No. I kept walking unmolested and an hour and a half later I reached my neighbor. He had heard the wolves but, of course, hadn't realized that they had surrounded me. In any event, he lent me his gun and a dozen cartridges. I began to retrace my journey.

Now that I was armed, I was no longer afraid. Instead, I was angry with the wolves. They had thoroughly terrified me and I was going to avenge myself by killing them—or so I thought.

When I got back to my logging area some three hours after leaving it, however, the wolves had gone. But there were many, many tracks—big paw prints. When I measured them later, I found they were three and a half inches wide and five inches long.

HOW BIG IS A WOLF TRACK?

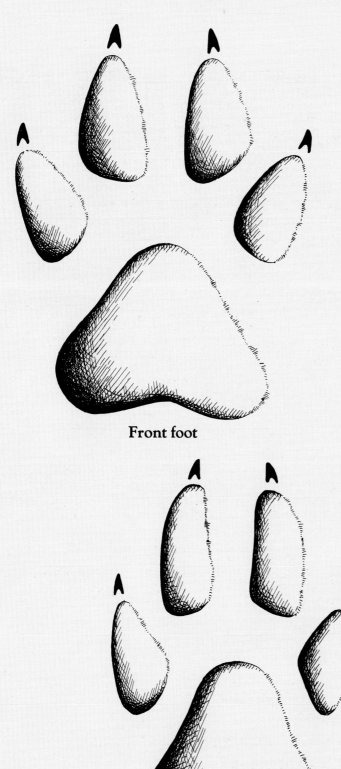

Front foot

Back foot

The answer to this question depends upon (1) the size of the wolf that left the track; (2) whether it was running, leaping, or walking; (3) the surface over which it was moving. Just as big humans usually have big feet, so big wolves have feet to match.

If an average wolf is walking on firm ground, it leaves front-foot tracks that measure about 4$\frac{1}{2}$ inches long by 3$\frac{3}{4}$ inches wide, and back-foot tracks that are about 4 inches long by 3 inches wide. If a wolf is running, especially over mud, sand, or snow, its weight will cause the toes to spread, and its tracks will be larger—perhaps up to 5 inches long by 4$\frac{1}{2}$ inches wide for the front feet and up to 4$\frac{1}{2}$ inches long by 4 inches wide for the back feet.

Following tracks that led from my log pile to an area of forest where the trees grew so close together that from a short distance away I could not see through them, I found a patch of bloody snow. A moment after, I saw the leg bone of a deer and soon the remains of the whole animal—a gory and grisly sight. Its head had been removed from the neck and most of its skin was torn off. It made me shudder. "That might be *my* head lying there," I thought.

Only later, in the safety of my home, did I then realize what had really happened. Evidently, the wolves had just killed the deer when I arrived. The remains were only twenty yards from where I had prepared to cut down the tree.

Wolves express hostility in subtle and sometimes not so subtle ways.

11

Wolves often howl to establish their territory.

Understandably, the hungry wolves had not wanted my company! They had howled and barked and circled me, and they had scared me away. They had *bluffed* me! Then they had gone back to finish their meal. When I figured this out, I realized that the wolves had not intended to attack me. All they had wanted was to be left in peace.

That experience taught me not to be afraid of wolves and, indeed, led me to make a study of them. Today, thirty-five years later, I know that most of these highly intelligent animals seldom attack humans, that they usually live peacefully among themselves when they are not molested, and that they kill only what they want to eat.

Now, after studying fifty-one wild packs and personally raising four pups, I have concluded that wolves are greatly misunderstood animals that play an important role in the wilderness.

The leader of the pack
emerges from the woods.

Wolves of North America

The ancestors of wolves first appeared on earth about five million years ago. They were large, meat-eating animals whose fossil bones have been found in many parts of the world. Scientists believe that those powerful, prehistoric mammals evolved to become the wolves that we know today.

Although wolves are found in most of the northern parts of the world, including Europe and Asia, this book concentrates on the two species of wolves that live in North America, from Mexico to the Arctic—the gray, or timber, wolf (whose scientific name is *Canis lupus*) and the red wolf (*Canis niger*). The gray wolf has twenty-seven subspecies, which include the white Arctic wolf. The subspecies may differ from one another in size, weight, and/or color, depending upon what part of the world they come from.

No two wolves look exactly alike. Some wolves are all black except for a white mark on their chests. Arctic wolves are all white. Others may be a combination of gray, white, fawn, black, and brown. People who study wolves soon learn to identify each animal by the markings on its fur, which are unique.

The red wolf, now found only in small numbers in the southwestern United States, almost became extinct because of persecution and changes made in its environment by humans. Its former range was from southern Pennsylvania to the Gulf of Mexico and south into Florida. However, by 1970, only a few red wolves were known to exist in one area along the Texas-Louisiana Gulf coast. Numbers of them have been bred in captivity and released in

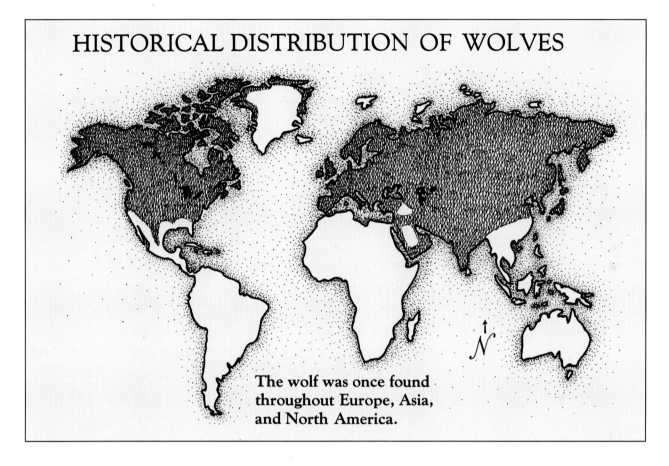

HISTORICAL DISTRIBUTION OF WOLVES

The wolf was once found throughout Europe, Asia, and North America.

parts of their original range by the U.S. Fish and Wildlife Service. These efforts may save the red wolf from extinction.

Adult wolves weigh from fifty-seven pounds to a record of more than one hundred seventy pounds, depending on where they live. An average weight for a male is about eighty-eight pounds, and about eighty-one pounds for a female. The largest wolves are found in the Northwest Territories, the Yukon Territory, and Alaska. Red wolves are somewhat smaller than gray wolves and seldom weigh more than seventy-five pounds. The smallest North American wolves live in Mexico.

Wolves are only found today in most of the northern parts of the world, including Greece, Spain, China, the Soviet Union, and North America.

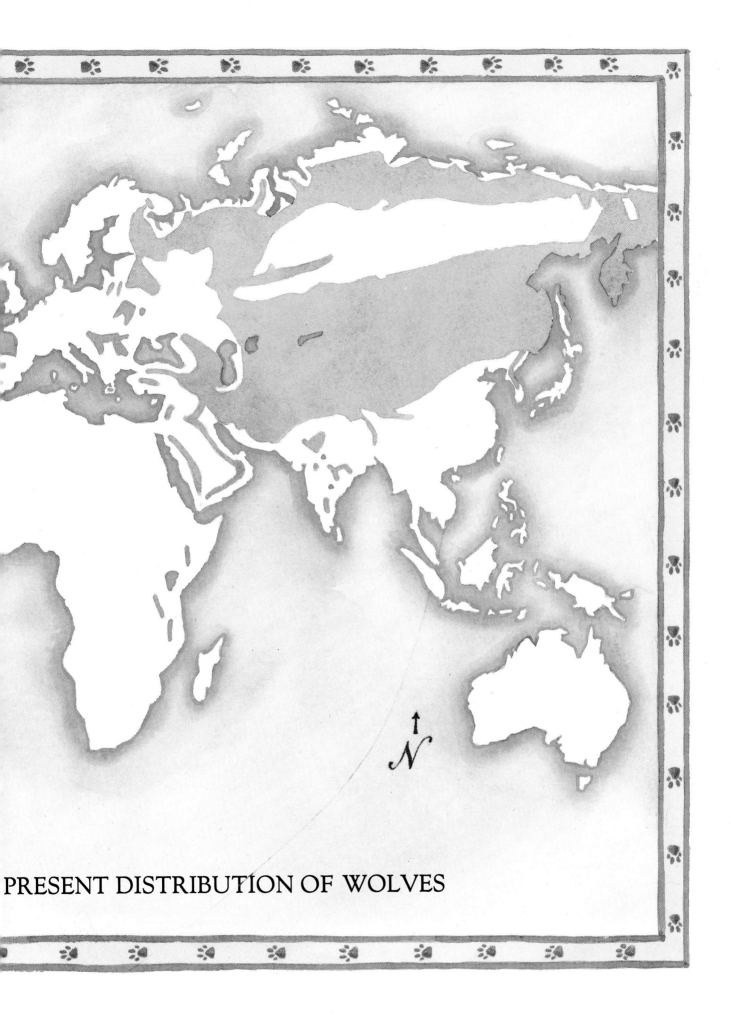

PRESENT DISTRIBUTION OF WOLVES

The length of a wolf is between fifty-nine and eighty inches. A large gray wolf may be thirty-six inches tall at the shoulder.

Biologists are often asked how long wolves live. That is an impossible question to answer for wild wolves. In captivity, wolves have been known to live up to seventeen years, but life in the wild is hard and it may be a really lucky wolf that can live for nine or ten years.

The gray wolf species includes wolves that have black fur.

For centuries, there have been frightening legends about wolves. Until fairly recently, people even believed in werewolves—humans that changed into wolves and attacked people. Such myths came from imaginative humans who feared wolves and saw them as powerful enemies.

Unlike Europeans, who hated wolves and were afraid of them, the native people of North America respected these animals. The Pawnees of Kansas and Nebraska, who named the stars after the animals with whom they shared the environment, called a star The Wolf. The Cree of Canada called the wolf *Mak-eh-coon* and believed that heavenly wolves visited the earth when the Northern Lights shone in winter.

The red wolf is nearly extinct and the U.S. Fish and Wildlife Service has bred a number in captivity. By releasing young wolves in their former range, they hope to re-establish the species.

Many Native Americans named themselves after the wolf, not just because they admired the animal, but also because they were impressed by its strength, courage, and ability to hunt, and by the close family ties that exist among wolf packs. Many also believe that wolves howl after they have eaten their fill to invite ravens, gray jays, chickadees, mice, foxes, and coyotes to come and share their food.

Indian medicine men often prayed to the wolf when they were curing a patient, sometimes

The length of a gray wolf ranges from fifty-nine to eighty inches

IS IT A WOLF OR A COYOTE?

WOLF

COYOTE

Coyotes are usually smaller than wolves and have larger ears and shorter muzzles.

howling, at other times calling directly to the wolf, asking his spirit to enter the sick person and to give him or her the strength to fight the evil spirits that had taken charge of the body.

In some parts of North America, coyotes (*Canis latrans*) are often called "brush wolves," but this is a misnomer. Coyotes are actually very different from their wild cousins in size, appearance, and habits. For example, the largest coyotes are about the same size as the smallest wolves. And the coyotes' life-style is very different. When coyote pups grow up, they usually leave their parents, so coyotes do not live in social groups as wolves do.

The New Generation

In the southern parts of their range, wolves mate in February, usually about the middle of the month. The pups are born some sixty-three days later, in late April or early May, depending upon when the mother became pregnant. In the far north, because of the colder climate, mating usually takes place during March, and most pups are born in late May or early June, when the weather is warmer.

Wolf puppies come into the world with their eyes shut and almost entirely helpless. Their faces are blunt, their back legs are not yet properly developed, their ears are almost stuck to their heads, and their tails are short and spindly. At birth they

Three young gray wolf pups curl up together in their snug den.

22

are between eight and nine inches long, including their short tails, and they weigh about a pound. Most are born wearing a brown coat of fine wool, but sometimes a puppy will have a dark, bluish coat and will grow up to be black all over, except for a white patch on its chest.

Before the pups are born, the mother wolf digs out a den, or nesting chamber, under the floor of the forest and a tunnel to reach it. The tunnel may be as short as three yards or as long as ten. Sometimes the mother wolf is helped by other females of the pack.

When the mother is close to giving birth and is

Red wolf pups enjoy their mother's milk. This family is being raised in captivity.

resting inside the chamber, the other wolves gather outside the entrance. They howl, as though they were singing to her, and they sniff at the den entrance, for even if the tunnel is long and twisting, the wolves' keen noses can tell at once when the first pup is born. All of them are excited as they await the arrival of the new generation.

In the nesting chamber, the mother wolf shows signs of pain. She whines now and then and licks herself a great deal. After a time, the first puppy emerges.

The wolves gathered outside of the tunnel entrance become even more excited and sing loudly, wagging their tails furiously. In between howls they sniff and lick one another and dance. It looks as if they are smiling as they celebrate the arrival of each newborn.

The puppy, still attached to its mother by the birth cord, lies helpless on the den floor, its mouth opening and shutting slowly as it takes its first gasps of air. The mother now leans toward it and bites off the cord close to the pup's abdomen. The little wolf usually gives a squeak of pain, and a droplet of blood emerges from the small wound, which will soon heal and become the pup's navel. The mother comforts the baby, licking away the blood and afterbirth membrane. Then, because the wolfling is soaking wet, she licks it dry with her long, wide tongue.

A young wolf gives its sibling a playful bite on the back of the neck. An adult wolf would discipline a young pup in the same way.

When the puppy is dry, the mother pushes it toward her milk-filled nipples. Soon, while the newcomer is enjoying its first meal, another pup is born, and the mother wolf turns her attention to it. A wolf mother usually gives birth to five or six pups, but she may have only one or as many as twelve.

While the mother feeds and cares for the little pups, the father and other members of the pack bring her meat. They keep her well fed at a time when she cannot leave the den to hunt, yet needs a lot of food in order to maintain her strength and produce milk for her babies.

Arctic wolf pups, like this one, are born in late May or early June when the weather is warmer in the far north.

*Two wolf pups playfully
nuzzle their parent.*

Exploring the World

Wolf puppies grow quickly, well nourished by their mother's rich milk. The first big event in their lives occurs when their eyes open, eleven to fifteen days after birth. The eyes are blue then and do not turn the deep yellow color so characteristic of wolf eyes until the pups are about three months old.

A few days after their eyes open, the small wolves become quite active, playing with one another, climbing over the adult animals, biting their tails and ears, making small growls and reedy little howls. They can become something of a nuisance to the big wolves, but the adults are patient. If a wolf

A feather becomes a handy toy for this Arctic wolf pup.

Wolf cubs emerge from the den when they are three to four weeks old.

lies down in the shade to rest after a long hunt, only to be pestered by a pup or two, it merely gets up and stretches out in another place.

The pups still get milk from their mother, but at four weeks old, they are starting to eat meat and to gnaw on bones brought home by the members of the pack.

Now the mother, accompanied by the entire pack, leads her family away from the den, taking them to a previously chosen place where they will spend the next two or more months. Such places usually are open, grassy country surrounded by forest. Probably there are a number of boulders scattered around the open land, a stream or lake

Four pups sit in the shelter of the rocks to wait for their parents to return from a hunt.

nearby so that the wolves can quench their thirst during the summer heat, and lots of shrubbery. Biologists call such a place a "resting area," or a *rendezvous*, from a French word that means "meeting place." The rendezvous is a summer sanctuary where the pups begin to practice the ways of wolves and where the adult members of the pack gather each day, guarding and supervising the young and resting before they have to set off on the hunt in early evening.

Led by an adult to a rendezvous, these pups explore their surroundings.

When the adult wolves are off hunting, one of their number stays behind as pup-sitter. Usually this is an adult female, perhaps an aunt, who looks after the young so the mother can get a well-earned rest or can hunt. If the pack has been successful, they announce their return to the young wolves and their sitter by howling when they are about a mile or so away from the rendezvous.

Long and echoing, the howls seem to fill the wilderness. An inexperienced human would have difficulty knowing the direction from which the calls

Wolves often howl to keep in touch with one another if some members of the pack are off hunting.

WHY DO WOLVES HOWL?

Wolves howl for many reasons. Sometimes they howl because they are happy; at other times to keep in touch, wolves also howl, especially when some members of the pack are off hunting. Or they howl to tell all their neighbors, "Keep out of my territory!" And they howl before they go hunting because they are excited and ready for the chase.

With their excellent hearing, wolves can pick up another wolf's howls over long distances—perhaps two to three miles away— especially when the wind is blowing in their direction.

Sometimes a wolf decides to leave its pack, look for a mate, and start a family of its own. The wolf announces its decision by long, somewhat sad-sounding howls that can be heard in January and February, throughout the breeding season. If another lone wolf of the opposite sex hears these lonely calls, it will immediately answer. Then, howling every now and then, each lone wolf trots toward the other, guided by the calls.

are coming, but the pups and their nurse quickly pinpoint it. Turning to face it, the little wolves and the adult reply, the young voices shrill and excitable, their guardian's deep and long-drawn.

The moment that the returning wolves enter the rendezvous, they are mobbed by the pups. One or two will go to the father, others to the mother. Whining with excitement, the young wolves nibble at the faces of the adults, stimulating an urge to bring up meat conveniently stored in the adult's stomach. The adult wolf arches its back, opens its mouth wide, and makes one or two coughing sounds. As it does so, a pup thrusts its muzzle right into the adult's mouth and is ready when the fresh, steaming meat comes up from the stomach and pops right into the young wolf's mouth.

An adult and a pup sniff with interest at a bit of fur.

These adult wolves have returned from a hunt ready to feed some hungry pups with regurgitated meat.

Wolves Go to School

The pups begin learning their wolf "ABCs" within a day or two of being born. At first, because they are small and weak, they teach themselves by always trying to outdo one another. They don't fight, but they struggle to get to their mother's back teats, which hold the most milk. They might also attempt to suck a neighbor's ear or tail. When they want to sleep, each tries to be the first to get to the warmest part of the mother's body, the place between her thighs. Such contests help them to coordinate their muscles and sharpen their wits.

Later, when they are old enough to leave the den, they play a lot, chasing one another, wrestling, pouncing on flowers, trying to catch flies, and sniffing at the many scents that surround them.

At about eight weeks old, the young wolves start to look more like their parents. The short tails of birth have grown long and thick, their noses are longer, and their ears stand up straight, looking too big for their heads. Their hind legs have lengthened and become strong.

The little wolves no longer need milk. Their first teeth are fully developed. Four fangs, two in each jaw, are long, thin, curved, and as pointed as needles. Now they practice hunting small animals, such as mice and voles, learning to listen for the faint rustling sounds made by the rodents as they travel through the long grasses.

The pups follow the sound of the small animals until they are near enough to smell them. When a pup gets very close to the scuttling rodent, it leaps into the air, landing an instant later, front feet first, paws aimed at the spot where it believes its prey is hiding. Lacking experience, a pup will miss often at first, but when it does land on the target, the rodent

Opposite:
This wolf pup is about eight weeks old.

36

A pup emerges from the den, ready to spend another day exploring his surroundings.

is immediately stunned. Then the successful wolfling snaps up its prize and runs, closely followed by its brothers and sisters, each of which will grab the prize if it can. These and many other activities are important parts of their education.

Soon the young wolves learn to count, wolf style. Wolves have amazing sensory memories, and because they study their world intently during every waking moment, they train themselves to remember everything they see, hear, or smell at any one time. For instance, if there are four large boulders near their den and one of them rolls away, the next day the wolves know that the boulders are not the same. It's not exactly counting as we define it, but wolves take account of everything in their environment.

Wolf pups investigate a new scent while their parents watch over them.

Wolf Senses

Like domestic dogs, wolves cannot recognize some stationary objects that are very far away. But they notice immediately any *movement* that may be a long way off—even the movement made by very small things, such as a fly landing on a flower several yards from them. Or they can spot a moose flicking its ears a great distance away.

Biologists say that wolves and dogs have poor *frontal* vision and superb *peripheral* vision. That means that although the wolf's eyes cannot recognize faraway objects, the *edges* of its eyes are quick to notice far-off movement, even if the wolf cannot tell what is making that movement. Humans,

Wolves have very sharp senses and can hear, see, and smell things that may be undetectable to humans.

birds, primates such as gorillas and chimpanzees, and a few other animals have good frontal vision.

Hearing—which for wolves is very keen—sight, and scent are all vital senses for wolves and other wild animals. The ability of wolves to detect even very faint smells from long distances away is almost unbelievable. One researcher discovered that a five-month-old wolf cub was able to pick up the smell of a porcupine eating grass in a meadow a mile from the cub!

A wolf digs up a supply of food that it buried for a future snack.

This young gray wolf investigates the curious new smells of the forest.

When the adult wolves lead the young away from their rendezvous, they allow them to play for a time, but soon they start to discipline the cubs, either by growling at them when they misbehave, or, if they are really naughty, by biting them in the loose skin at the back of the neck between the head and shoulders. Usually only one scruff bite is enough to teach the wolfling that school has started in earnest and that the business of learning to live in the wild is very serious indeed.

By early October the young wolves are losing all their baby teeth and replacing them with their permanent, adult set. Now they take their places in the pack as disciplined members of the hunt. They are still learning, of course, but they can help in the chase and even assist in making the final kill.

WOLF FACES

Normal Expression

Wolves seem to express their moods and feelings on their faces, much as people do. A wolf with its mouth half open and its eyes shining doubtless is indicating that it is happy. When young wolves are playing tag and chasing each other at full speed, or pretending to fight and rolling over and over on the ground, they look as if they are silently laughing. Their lips are pulled back, corners curving up slightly, and their muzzles are not wrinkled. Only the tips of their fangs are showing.

Apologetic

Happy

"I'm prepared to defend myself" or "I'm angry"

The Wolf Pack

Wolves usually occupy a rendezvous until late September or early October, when the pups are about five months old. At this time the young ones look almost exactly like their parents, but are about half the adult length and weigh between forty-five and fifty-five pounds. By now, all the members of the pack are growing their winter coats, which consist of long, shiny outer hairs called *guard hairs*, and an undercoat of thick, soft wool that is entirely waterproof. When their new coats are fully grown, wolves look much heavier and bigger than they actually are because of the thick winter fur.

The size of a wolf pack is determined by such things as the number of animals in its territory that can be caught; the kind of prey, like moose or deer; the age of the adult wolves; their state of health; and whether they are being trapped or hunted by humans. So a pack may be made up of as few as two or as many as twenty wolves. An average pack has about six or seven members. A pack is similar to a human family, for generally it consists of a father and mother wolf (the leaders), perhaps an uncle and an aunt, and several young wolves, usually brothers and sisters.

Pack numbers go up and down. Death reduces, birth increases them. Sometimes a young wolf will leave a pack to set up his own family with a lone female from a neighboring pack. At times, although seldom, a lone wolf from another pack will be accepted by neighboring wolves.

Some people believe that wolves overpopulate themselves. Not so; nature controls wolf numbers in many ways. If humans have not trapped or shot members of a pack, only the male and female leaders will breed. Any other adult wolves that show signs

A pack of Arctic wolves wanders across the tundra in search of prey.

of wanting to breed are quickly discouraged by the leaders. Newborn wolf pups are delicate in their first few weeks of life and many of them die—often even before their eyes open. Accidents and hunting injuries kill adult wolves. Also, wolves suffer from a number of illnesses and are almost never free of parasites, which can bring about disease and death.

The wolf pack turns toward the sound of an animal moving in the forest.

WHO LEADS THE WOLF PACK?

A wolf pack is like a traditional human family. There is the father, called the *Alpha* male, and the mother, called the *Alpha* female. Then there are aunts and uncles and new generation brothers and sisters.

The numbers in any pack vary. Some packs may have as many as twenty members, while others may have only two or three. The father and mother wolves—usually the most experienced—are in charge of the pack. The word *dominant* does not mean that the leaders are tyrants; it simply means that these leaders guide the family, determine when they should hunt, select the rendezvous and the home territory, lead the hunt, and charge to the front if they must defend the young wolves against bears or other predators. The leaders have the most responsibility and usually face the most dangers themselves.

Leaders respect the other members of their pack and are themselves respected. If an Alpha wolf must discipline a subordinate, it does so by growling, baring its shiny fangs, and now and then giving the offender a painless nip in the scruff of the neck.

Autumn seems to be the wolves' favorite season. They find the flies of spring and summer bothersome and the heat oppressive, especially before they have shed their winter coats in the spring. So, by fall, as the flies die and the days become sunny but cool, all the members of the wolf pack become excited and happy. They howl a great deal, and they charge around, running as fast as twenty-five miles an hour for short distances. Or they lope through the wilderness, inspecting their territory, at a rate of about seven and a half miles an hour. This is a speed that they can maintain for many hours without tiring or resting.

Such journeys may appear to be aimless, but those who study wolves think the wolves undertake them so that the young ones can learn all the boundaries of their home range. At certain places, the pack, following the example of the male and female leaders, stop to leave their scent on an old, rotting tree stump or a rock or a fallen tree. Males wet by raising one leg; females usually squat or sometimes raise a leg. The places they mark are called "scent stations."

Some biologists believe that the spots are marked regularly in order to warn other packs that the territory is already occupied by a wolf family. Also, it may be that scent stations are like post offices, where wolves can learn about other wolves simply by smelling their scent.

Spring in Alaska brings
warmer weather, melts much
of the snow, and carries new
scents.

Overleaf:
A wolf pack is similar to a
human family. It numbers
from two to twenty. The
average pack has six or seven
members.

The Life of a Hunter

Wolves are predators—animals that catch other animals for food. But they like some kinds of animals better than others. Of course, if a wolf is really very hungry, it will eat almost anything. Nevertheless, most wolves hunt for what biologists call *preferred prey*. This means that they always try to catch those animals whose meat they have eaten and enjoyed as puppies. Probably they are much like us, who tend to prefer the kind of food we became used to when we were growing up.

If young wolves have been fed moose meat by their parents, they probably will hunt moose when they are grown up. But if moose are not available, they will hunt other animals, such as deer, elk, caribou, mountain goats, or beaver, depending on where they live.

Some people have said that wolves will survive by eating mice if no other food is available, but it is unlikely that these large wild animals could survive on a diet of mice alone. They tend to eat them on occasion, but only as a nibble. They need and they go after larger prey. When their chosen animals leave one part of the wilderness for another, the wolves follow.

The life of a wild hunter is hard. Wolves and other predators often have to go hungry for days at a time. They must run long distances through harsh terrain after moose, elk, caribou, deer—all of which are usually able to run faster than their hunters. Moose and deer, the generally preferred prey, can kill the wolves by stabbing them with their sharp front hooves. Wolves also risk injury when they chase through the forest at high speed, jumping over tangled dry branches that can seriously injure or kill them if they pierce a vital part of their bodies.

SKULL AND TEETH OF A WOLF

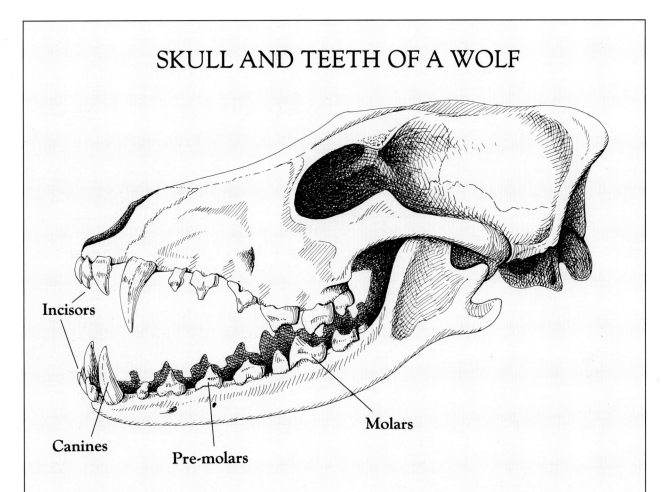

Incisors

Canines

Pre-molars

Molars

The structure of the wolf's head is broad from where it joins the neck up to the eyebrows. The part that contains the eyes, nose, and teeth tapers gradually, like the muzzle of a German shepherd, but it is wider.

Wolf bones are strong and heavy, especially those in the jaws, and they are powered by tough muscles. The wolf's jaws can exert great pressure.

Wolves have about twenty teeth in each jaw. At the front of the upper jaw there are six *incisors*, similar to our front teeth.

Next to them on either side are the *canines*, or fangs. Fangs may be as long as $1^1/2$ inches. Behind the canines are four pre-molars and two molars in the upper jaw, and four pre-molars and three molars in the lower jaw.

Each tooth has a very special purpose. The strong incisors are used like knives to cut off pieces of meat and to gnaw bones. The fangs are used for catching and holding prey, or for defense against other animals. The pre-molars and molars are used for chewing food.

WOLF PREY

Wolves prefer to hunt hoofed animals, such as musk oxen, deer, moose, and caribou, but they will also hunt beavers, rabbits, hares, and small rodents.

A study at Isle Royale, Michigan, where wolves and moose have been contending since the 1940s, showed that the wolves had to make about thirteen chases before they could kill one moose. Other studies have shown that when a moose refuses to run away from the wolves, they will not attack it. Instead, they lie around it for a while, now and then making charges at the big animal; if after about half an hour the moose still refuses to run, the wolf pack goes away in search of other prey.

Wolves must run long distances after prey.

AVOIDING A FIGHT

Wolves signal each other with their bodies, tails, and hair, as well as with their faces and voices. When a high-ranking wolf goes up to another wolf, or is approached by a lower-ranking pack member, it holds its tail up. If the signaling wolf is aggressive, it will hold its tail very high, and then its hackles will rise from the base of the tail almost to the very top of its head, making it look much larger than it really is. At the same time, the wolf arches its back and straightens and stiffens its legs, so that it moves almost as though it were walking on stilts.

Needless to say, the aggressive wolf is pretty frightening to see. A subordinate wolf will probably flop down on the ground, bend its head back to expose its throat, tuck its tail tightly between its legs, and lift the back leg that is not resting on the ground. These signals tell the other wolf that the subordinate animal does not want to fight.

Though the aggressive wolf knows that the other one is helpless and can easily be killed, it does not often attack. It seems to be satisfied by what one may call an apology from the opponent.

Normal position

Threatening

Imposing

Confident

People sometimes pity the hunted animal and then become angry at the hunter. They need to understand that predators, such as wolves, play an important role in the conservation of the natural world. Though at times they do kill healthy adult animals, mostly they kill the old or the sick or the weak. When the old, sick, and weak prey animals are killed, the healthy survivors have more room and more food.

Other people believe that wolves are cruel and enjoy torturing the animals they are about to kill. But to delay killing an animal in order to "torture" it would be inefficient. And wolves try to hunt as efficiently as possible.

Many other wilderness inhabitants benefit from the animals the wolves kill. While the wolves are eating, ravens and gray jays dart down from their perches and grab bits of the meat. During the winter, when the wolves have gone to rest some distance from their food, porcupines, snowshoe hares, weasels, mice, voles, squirrels, and little birds like chickadees, nuthatches, and woodpeckers come to feed on the leftovers. In the frost-free seasons, when there is little left except bones and bits of skin, flies and butterflies, beetles, worms of various kinds, and the microscopic creatures called bacteria all dine on the remains. At the same time, the blood and body juices of the dead animal and the droppings of the small animals and birds that feed on it enrich the soil and give life to seedling plants. It is truly said that when the wolf eats, everybody eats.

*A wolf tackles a large musk
ox.*

Under Northern Skies

When winter comes to the northland, it brings heavy snow and biting cold that often sends the thermometer down to 45 degrees below zero. Sometimes the moon shines and the northern lights cast their greenish flashes over the land, but this is a cold and dark time. In the tundra of northern Canada, where the barren-ground caribou live and where there are hardly any tall trees, the wind sweeps across the great open spaces and swirls the snow in all directions. Then the wolves curl up in their snow beds and stay there until the wind stops blowing.

A calm comes and eight or nine snowy mounds suddenly explode. From each naturally made igloo, a wolf emerges, shakes itself to get rid of the caked snow, and joins its companions in a long howl. Led by the leader male, the wolves sing their wild songs for several minutes, and all the animals who hear their chorus will know that the wolf pack is hungry and about to seek a meal.

Moments after the last echoes of their voices disappear in the frozen distance, the wolves trot away, heads up, noses testing the wind for the scent of the food that they need. Trotting tirelessly over the tundra, the North American wolves behave exactly as generations of their kind behaved thousands of years ago.

Wind and snow sweep across the tundra, but Arctic wolves are well adapted to their inhospitable environment.

This wolf is alert to movement and sounds of potential prey.

We are gradually coming to understand that predators, such as wolves, have an essential role in the conservation of the natural world. Biologists have learned to study them in their natural habitat and, in some cases, have been able to watch them for long periods of time. As a result, the old myths and fears about wolves are dying. Wolves deserve to live undisturbed and we should ensure that they will.

The wolves prepare to continue their journey through the snow.

INDEX

Numbers in italics refer to photographs.

WITHDRAWN